contents

How to Draw

by

Helen Webster

Schools Library and Information Services

Arcturus Publishing Ltd
26/27 Bickels Yard
151–153 Bermondsey Street
London SE1 3HA

Published in association with
foulsham
W. Foulsham & Co. Ltd,
The Publishing House, Bennetts Close, Cippenham,
Slough, Berkshire SL1 5AP, England

ISBN 0-572-02883-0

British Library Cataloguing-in-Publication Data: a catalogue record for this
book is available from the British Library

Editor: Rebecca Panayiotou
Text design: Viki Ottewill
Cover design: Stünkel Studio

Printed in China

introduction

This book works on the idea that anything and everything that you could want to draw can be broken down into simple geometric shapes, like circles and squares. All you have to do is follow the simple step-by-step instructions until you have accurately built up the basic shape of the object that you want to draw.

With this in mind, I think that this book can be used in 3 different ways…

1

You can follow each clear step, building up the image lightly in pencil. Then when the outline is complete, you can go over the image in pen, like so:

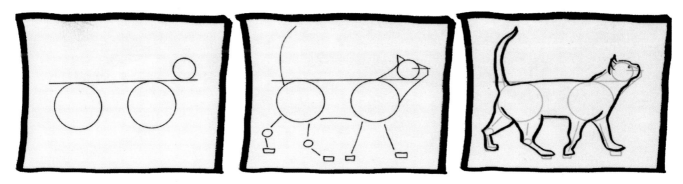

2

You can draw out the shape on a piece of paper, then get some tracing paper, place it on top and use the image underneath as a guide to your final drawing.

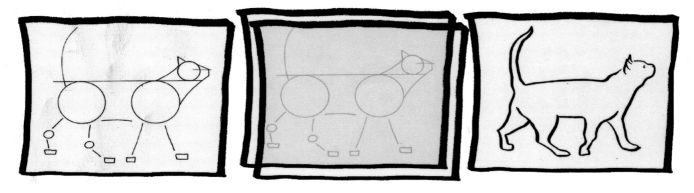

3

You can simply use the book as a helpful reference for when you are drawing any animal, person or object that is in front of you.

how to draw a dinosaur

First of all we are going to look at the basic shape of a brachiosaurus.

It has a squished circle for a body, a teeny circle for a head, and a long bendy neck and tail.

teeny circle

same length as tail

squished circle

about the width of 4 fingers

Next, we add the legs. The dinosaur's front legs are straight, while the back legs are slightly bent.

straight rectangular legs

back legs are jointed

Now all we need to do is join it up!

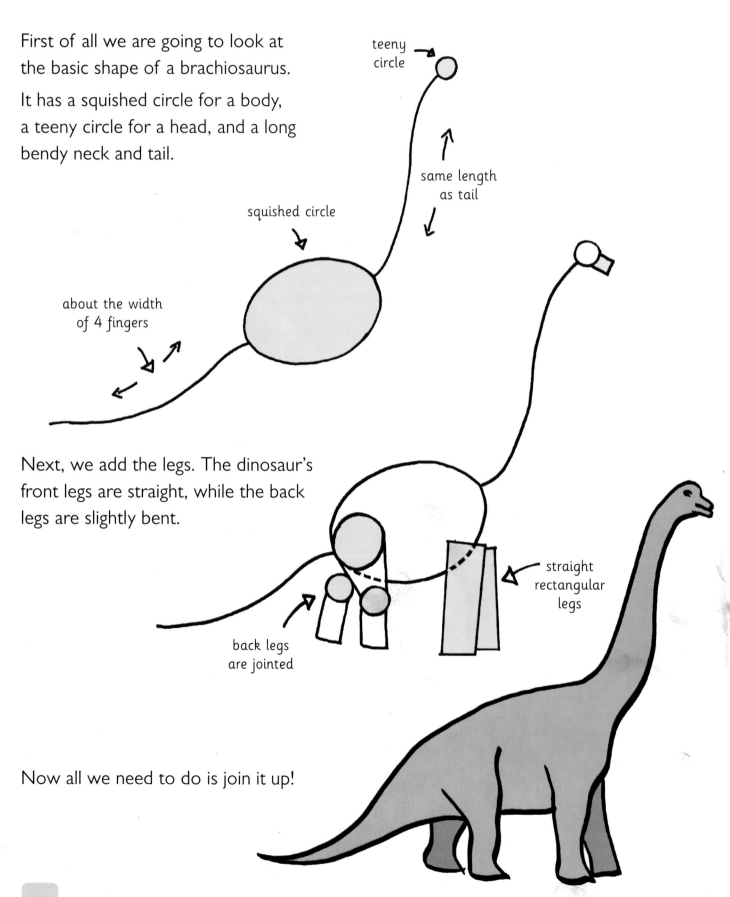

You can see that the tyrannosaurus is similar: a squished body, bent back legs, a long tail and a circle for a head.

the same squished circle is used to draw the body

To draw a dinosaur's head you draw a circle with a triangle and an oblong coming out from the side.

the head is made up of a circle, a triangle and an oblong

the eye goes here

a sausage for a neck

Dinosaurs always have lemon-shaped eyes and slits for nostrils.

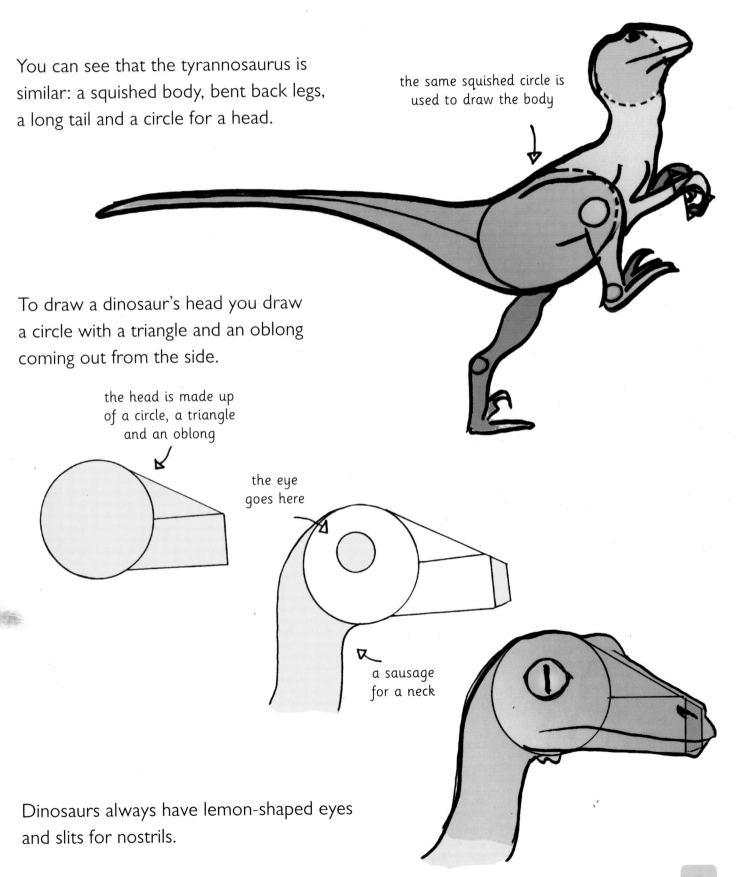

how to draw a horse

To draw a horse, first draw a wonky cross.

Then place four circles in the positions shown here.

Make sure that they all touch the cross.

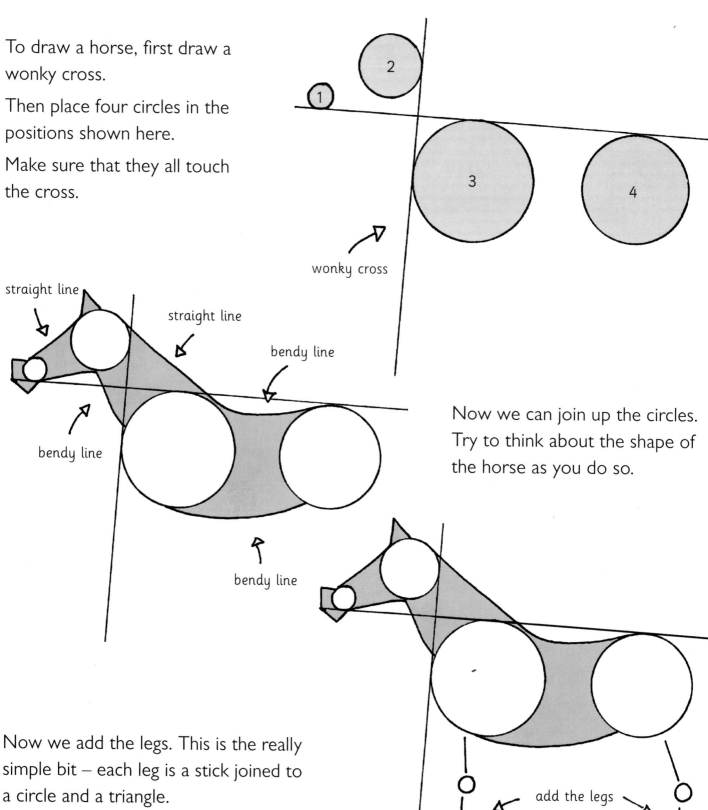

wonky cross

straight line

straight line

bendy line

bendy line

bendy line

Now we can join up the circles. Try to think about the shape of the horse as you do so.

Now we add the legs. This is the really simple bit – each leg is a stick joined to a circle and a triangle.

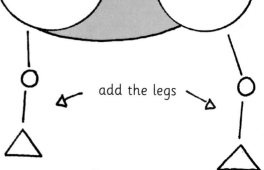

add the legs

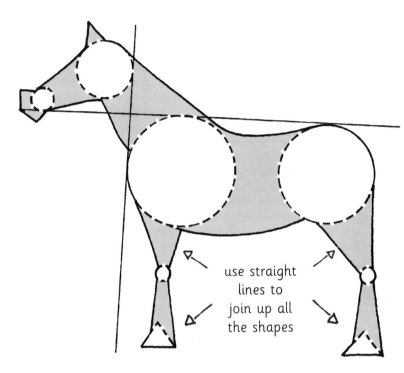

Finally, join the legs to the rest of the body. You should now be able to see the outline of the horse clearly.

use straight lines to join up all the shapes

Can you see the distinct shapes in the horse's body?

You will be able to use this technique every time you want to draw a horse.

how to draw a dog

A dog is made up of three circles. They all sit on a right angle.

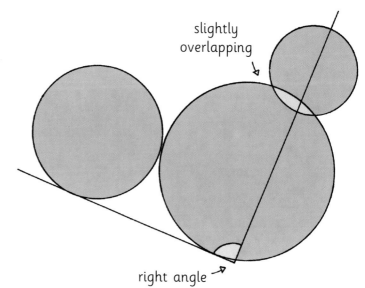

slightly overlapping

right angle

To define the body and head, add a triangle for the ear, a pointy rectangle for the nose and a zig-zag line for the belly.

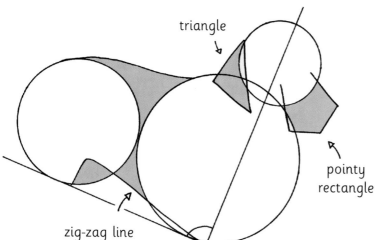

triangle

pointy rectangle

zig-zag line

The dog's front legs are straight lines but the hind legs are bent backwards.

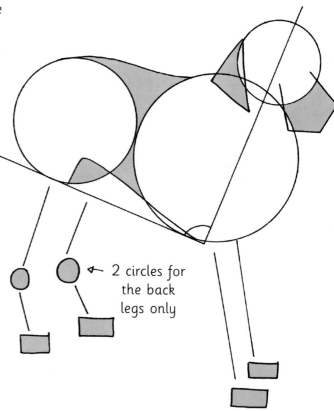

2 circles for the back legs only

This is always the last part – we join the legs to the rest of the body. Don't forget to add a tail!

tail

now draw lines to join up all the shapes

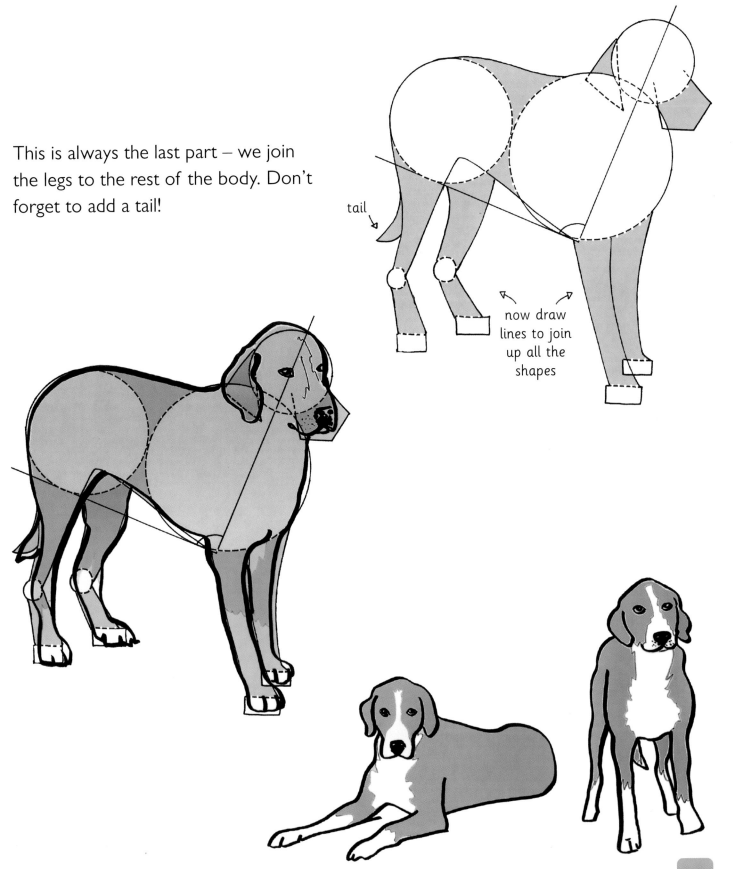

how to draw a cat

A cat's body is made up of two equal sized circles — spaced about a thumb's width apart — plus a small circle for the head.

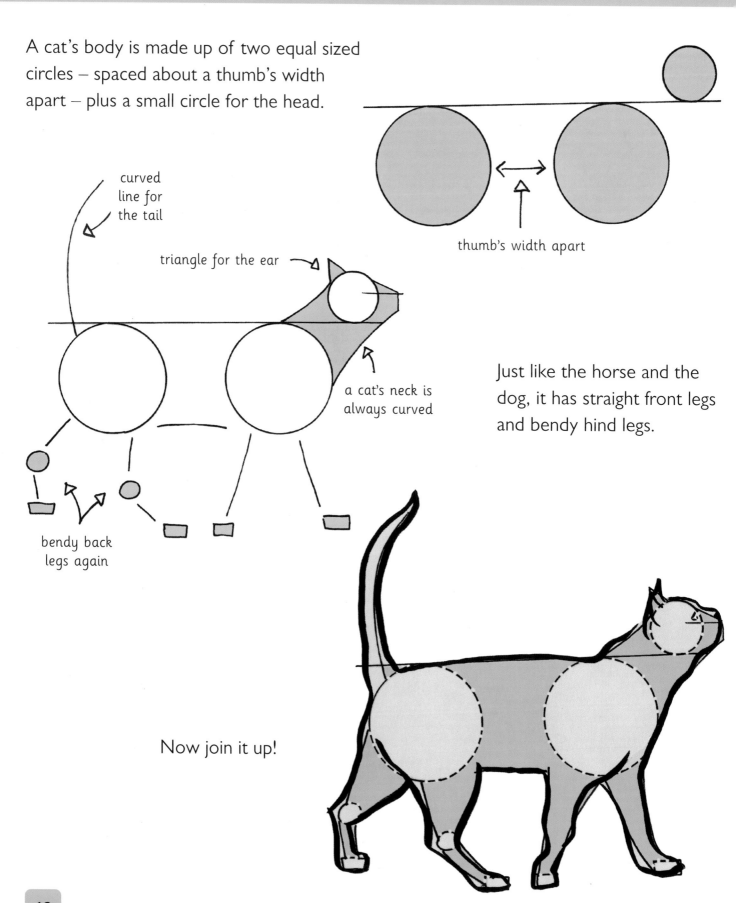

thumb's width apart

curved line for the tail

triangle for the ear

a cat's neck is always curved

bendy back legs again

Just like the horse and the dog, it has straight front legs and bendy hind legs.

Now join it up!

To draw its head, simply draw a circle with a line slicing into it — just above the centre. This is to line up the eyes and nose.

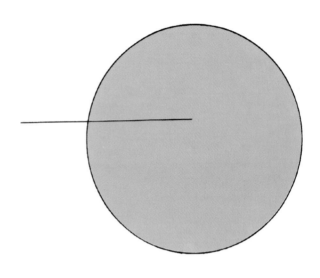

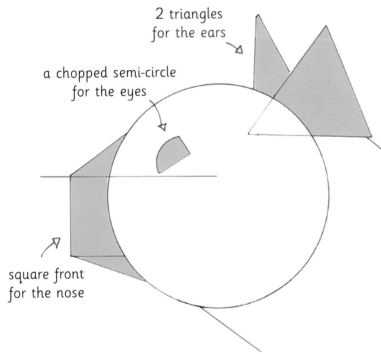

2 triangles for the ears

a chopped semi-circle for the eyes

square front for the nose

Now add two triangles for the ears, a chopped semi-circle for the eyes, and a square front for the nose.

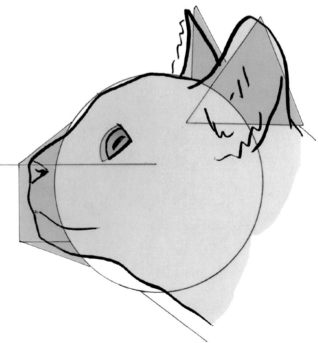

how to draw a bird

To draw a bird, first draw a big circle or egg shape.

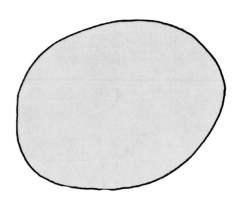

Now draw a line and a smaller egg shape for the neck and head.

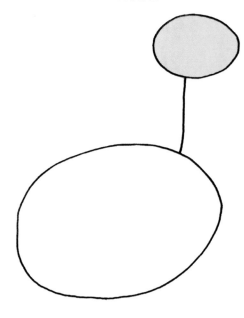

The feet are really simple. Use two tiny circles for the knees and three short lines for the feet. The knees tend to be quite high up.

Use triangles to give the bird a beak and tail feathers.

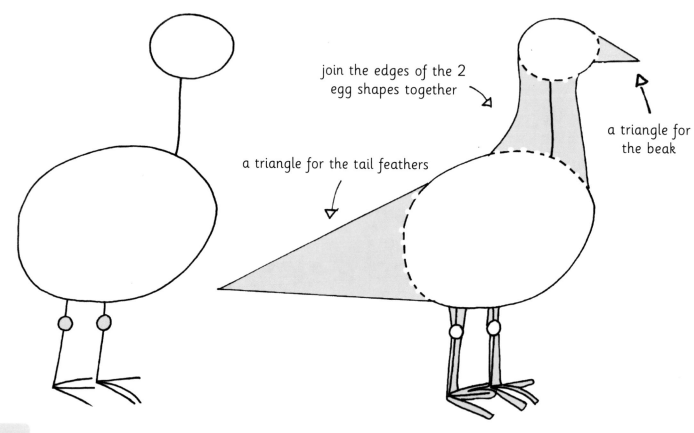

join the edges of the 2 egg shapes together

a triangle for the tail feathers

a triangle for the beak

like dinosaurs, birds have lemon-shaped eyes

add some wobbly lines to show that there are feathers

All birds are made up of one large and one small egg shape. The things that vary are the length of the neck and legs. So as long as you remember these rules, you'll never go wrong!

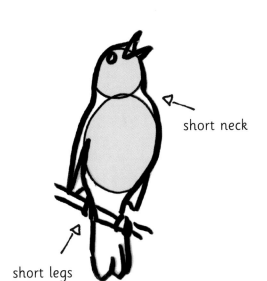

short neck

short legs

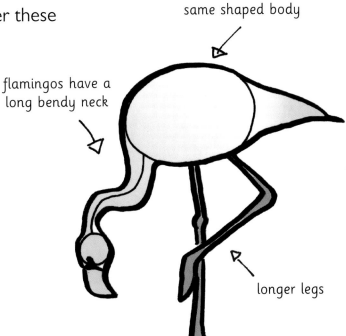

all birds have the same shaped body

flamingos have a long bendy neck

longer legs

how to draw a bird in flight

To draw a bird in flight, first draw your two egg shapes, with the smaller one facing in the direction that the bird is flying.

The tail always has a fan-like appearance. It's up to you whether the bird will have plumage or not. In this instance, it has a little.

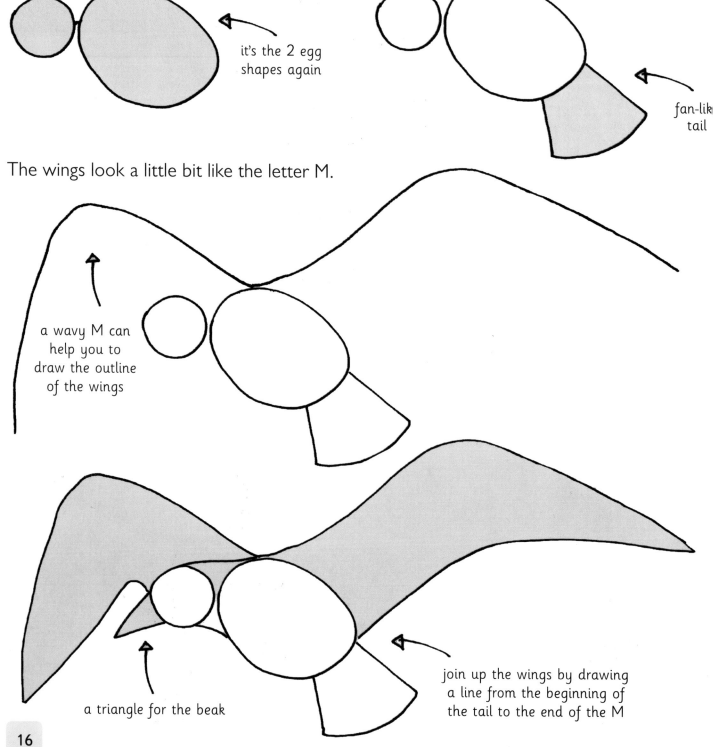

it's the 2 egg shapes again

fan-like tail

The wings look a little bit like the letter M.

a wavy M can help you to draw the outline of the wings

a triangle for the beak

join up the wings by drawing a line from the beginning of the tail to the end of the M

Just add the final touches!

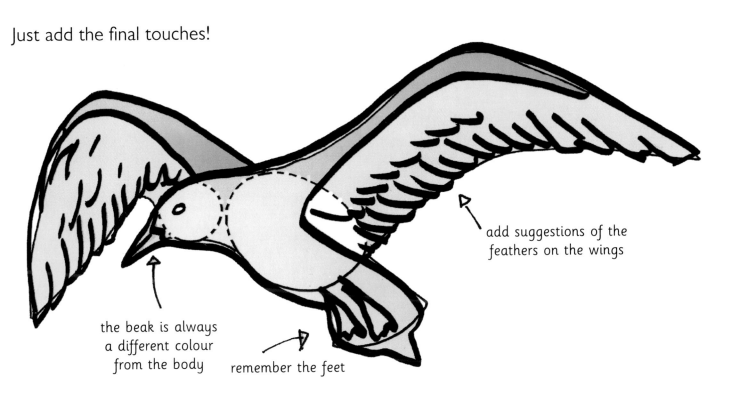

add suggestions of the feathers on the wings

the beak is always a different colour from the body

remember the feet

Experiment with bending or straightening the wings to show different stages of flight.

how to draw a plane

Planes are a little more complicated to draw than they look,
but actually a plane is just a torpedo with wings.

Whenever you start to draw a plane, always draw a cross first.
This will give you a rough idea of where everything will sit.

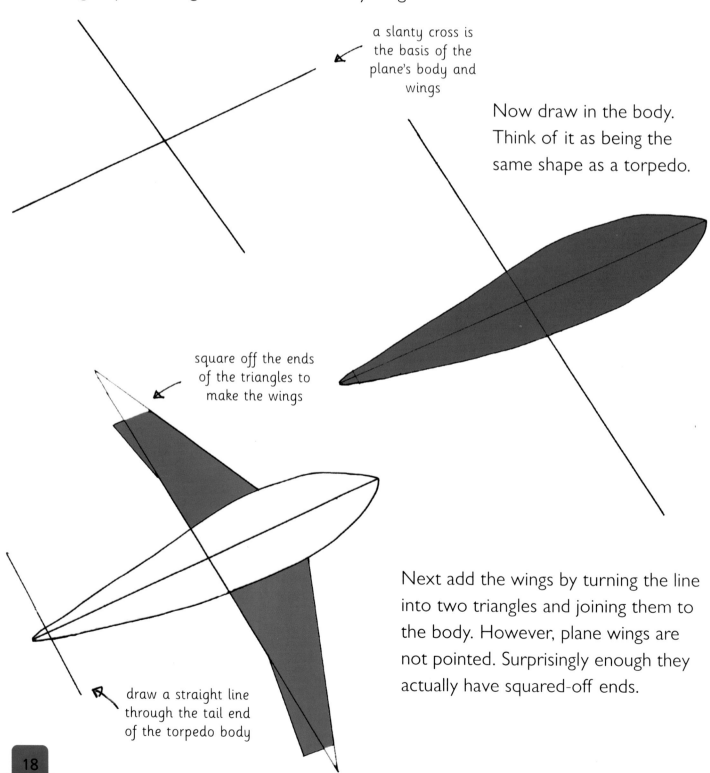

a slanty cross is
the basis of the
plane's body and
wings

Now draw in the body.
Think of it as being the
same shape as a torpedo.

square off the ends
of the triangles to
make the wings

Next add the wings by turning the line
into two triangles and joining them to
the body. However, plane wings are
not pointed. Surprisingly enough they
actually have squared-off ends.

draw a straight line
through the tail end
of the torpedo body

18

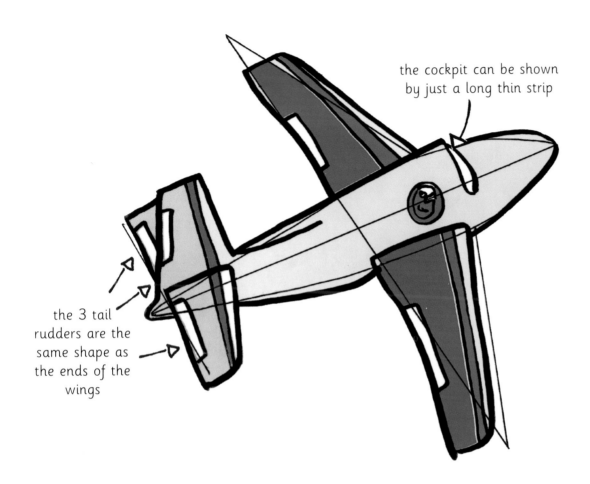

the cockpit can be shown by just a long thin strip

the 3 tail rudders are the same shape as the ends of the wings

Once you have the basics you can alter the body or the wings to make different kinds of aeroplanes. For example, a bigger body makes a jumbo jet while a larger pair of wings will give you a concorde or a jet fighter plane!

how to draw a car

First draw a straight horizontal line. Then draw two circles as shown.

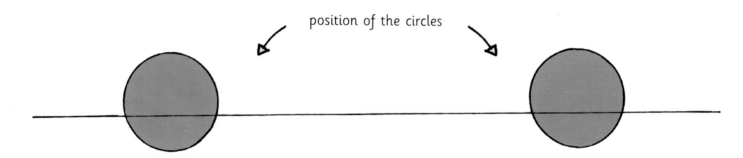

position of the circles

Now draw an oblong to show the general shape of the chassis. Use the horizontal line to show you where the bottom of the oblong sits.

the oblong

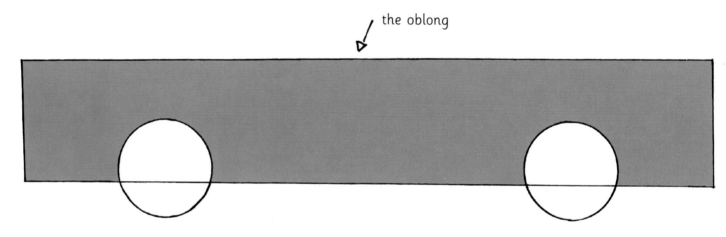

Draw a line from the top left-hand corner of the oblong to the edge of the wheel – halfway up that line is roughly where the roof of the car should begin.

a sloped mound is the roof of the car

the mound ends where the front wheel starts

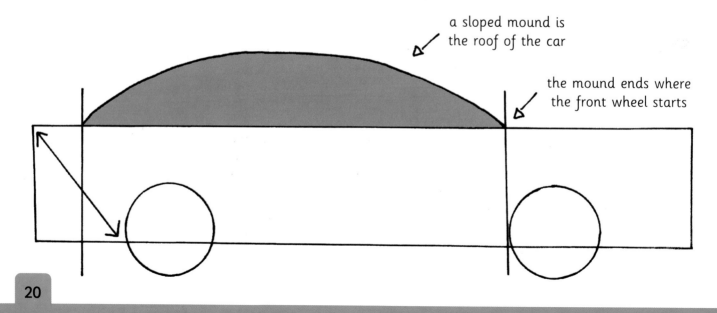

the bonnet is a curving line to the bottom right-hand corner of the oblong

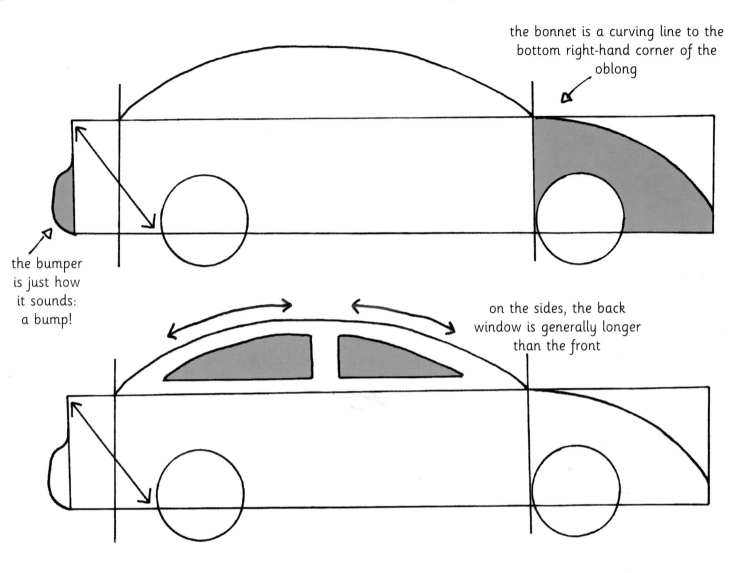

the bumper is just how it sounds: a bump!

on the sides, the back window is generally longer than the front

Use your imagination to decide what colour, wheels and features you would like. And then, hey presto, you have yourself a car!

how to draw a racing car

The thing to remember with cars is that they all have an oblong for a body. Some are pointed at the front, some have flaring spoilers at the back, but they still have the basic shape of an oblong with wheels.

because it needs to go very quickly, a racing car's chassis is very close to the ground

racing cars have their back wheel at the very end of the car

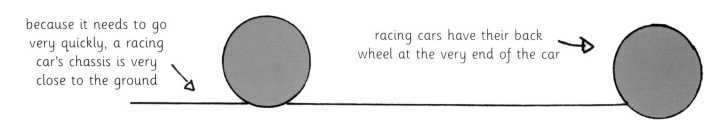

the same oblong shape is used for the car's chassis

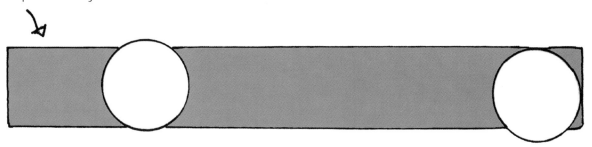

curved bonnet from the top of the front wheel to the bottom corner of the oblong

notice that there is only half of the curved top. The front part is missing

a rectangle for the spoiler

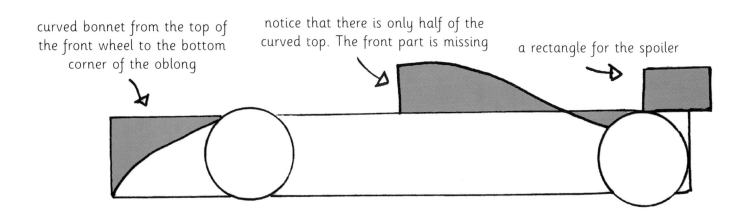

Colour the car with as many different colours as you can!

add your racing driver here!

Once you have mastered the basics of the motor car, it's really fun to experiment with different shapes and styles. Go on, design your own car! You can create some wacky or cool cars just by exaggerating one aspect, e.g. a curved bonnet or a pointed boot, or you could make a convertible by leaving off the roof! The ideas are endless…

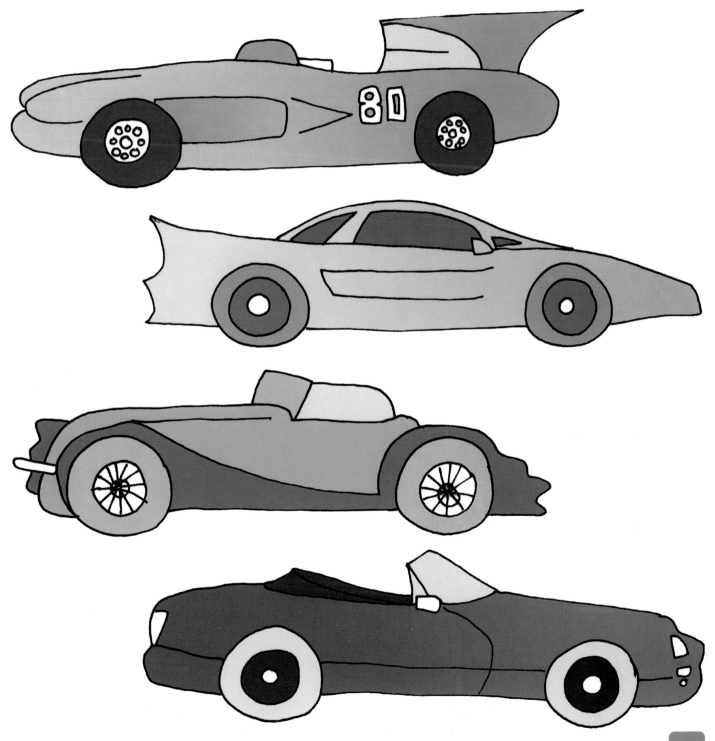

how to draw a head

To draw a head, first of all draw a cross.
Then place a circle slap bang in the middle.

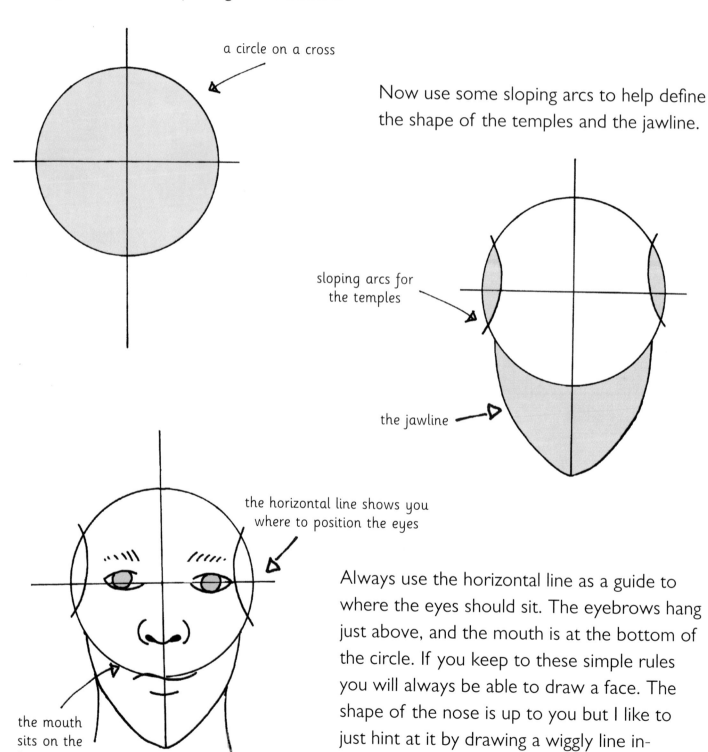

a circle on a cross

Now use some sloping arcs to help define the shape of the temples and the jawline.

sloping arcs for the temples

the jawline

the horizontal line shows you where to position the eyes

Always use the horizontal line as a guide to where the eyes should sit. The eyebrows hang just above, and the mouth is at the bottom of the circle. If you keep to these simple rules you will always be able to draw a face. The shape of the nose is up to you but I like to just hint at it by drawing a wiggly line in-between two brackets.

the mouth sits on the bottom of the circle

Don't forget the hair and ears – have fun experimenting with different shapes and styles.

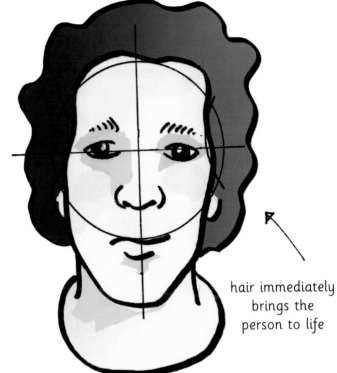

hair immediately brings the person to life

The three-quarter and side-on views are a bit more complicated. Just remember to use the cross and the circle as a guide to where the features sit.

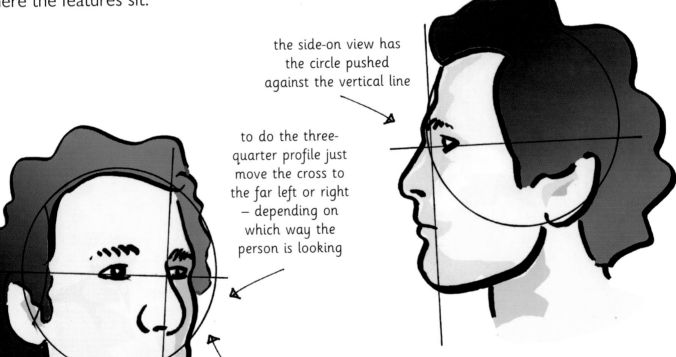

the side-on view has the circle pushed against the vertical line

to do the three-quarter profile just move the cross to the far left or right – depending on which way the person is looking

the eyes and mouth are still in the same place but the nose now has a sloping line going from the eyebrow to the far nostril

how to draw facial expressions

Just by altering the mouth and eyes, and nothing else, you can completely change the expression on someone's face. Look at the examples below. The shape of the face, the hair and the nose hardly change, but the face can look completely different just by widening the eyes, raising the eyebrows, adding some creases to the forehead or by changing the style of the mouth. You can literally wipe the smile off his face!

 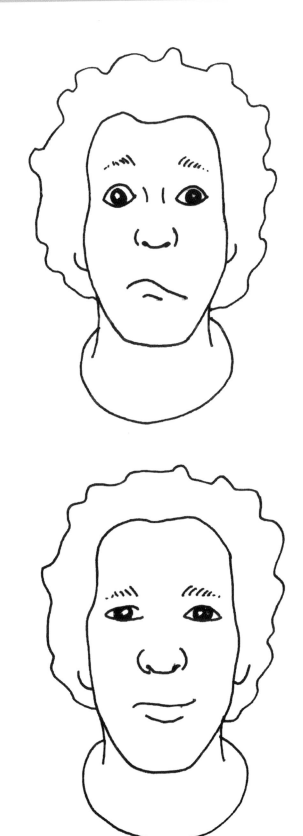

how to draw hands

Drawing hands is something that everyone dreads. I did too, until I found out about the arc and sausages idea.

Here's how it works: the palm of the hand can be drawn as if it is a right angled arc. Then each finger is just three small sausages hanging on to the end of each other, with each one getting a little smaller as they go.

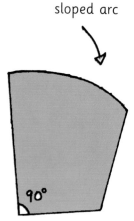

sloped arc

90°

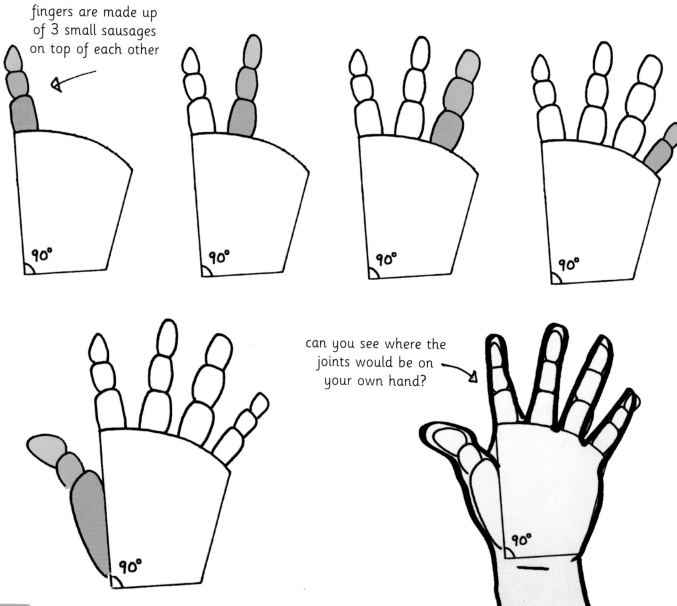

fingers are made up of 3 small sausages on top of each other

can you see where the joints would be on your own hand?

90° 90° 90° 90° 90° 90°

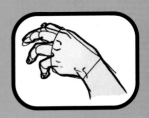

Remember that each sausage is very flexible and can bend an awful lot.

the same basic sloped arc shape for the hand

the 3 small sausages bent into different positions

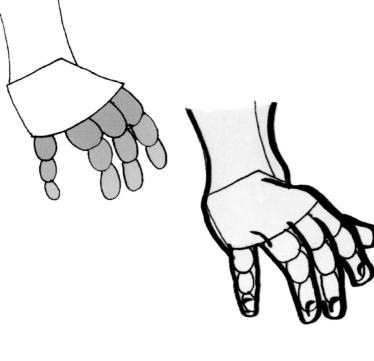

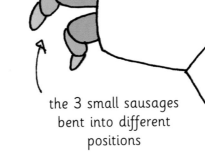

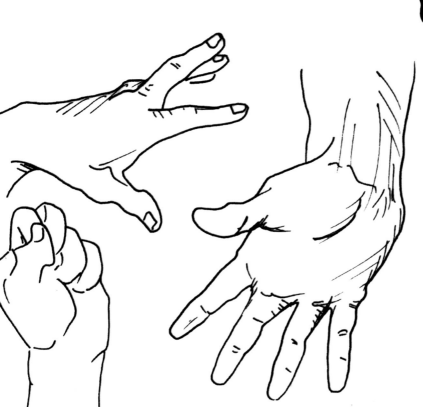

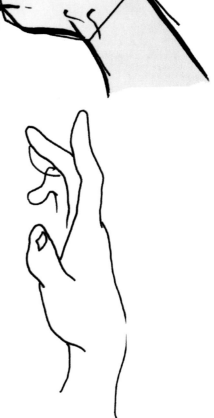

how to draw a child

First of all, look at how your model is standing. Usually, he or she is slightly bent to the left or right, so draw a curved line with a circle on top. The line should be as long as the body and legs. Now divide the body into four equal sections by drawing in four horizontal lines.

For the body, draw a squidgy rectangle. The top and bottom of the rectangle are the same width, but the sides look like they have been squeezed in. This is for the waist.

divide the body into 4 equal sections using 4 horizontal lines

a squidgy rectangle

Now draw circles where you want the elbows, knees and feet to be. Remember to use your dividing lines as a guide to where these should go.

Join all the shapes together.

pelvis — this is where the body ends and the legs begin

elbow joint

knee joint

ankle joint

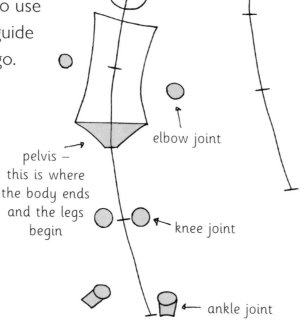

Finally, use the body frame to help you draw the clothes in the right places.

For the side view, the same principles apply: you have a curved line with four dividing lines – all an equal distance apart. If you remember this rule, you will be able to draw anyone doing anything!

← squidgy rectangle for a body

← always remember to use circles for the elbow, knee and ankle joints

← same 4 lines are used to show where the elbows, pelvis, knees and feet go

See if you can find the squidgy rectangle and joints on these children...

how to draw an adult

To draw an adult's body, start with your usual long curve and mark it with six dividing lines.

Now draw a small circle for the head (it starts at Line 1) and a squished circle for the bottom and hips (it sits on Line 4).

Next add the shoulders (at Line 2).

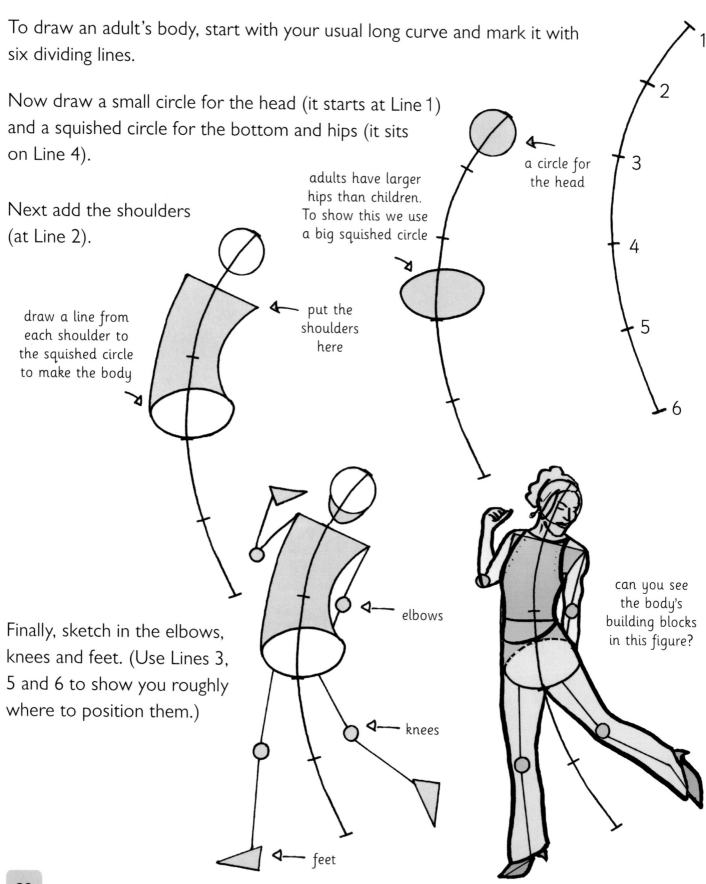

a circle for the head

adults have larger hips than children. To show this we use a big squished circle

put the shoulders here

draw a line from each shoulder to the squished circle to make the body

Finally, sketch in the elbows, knees and feet. (Use Lines 3, 5 and 6 to show you roughly where to position them.)

elbows

knees

feet

can you see the body's building blocks in this figure?

1
2
3
4
5
6

If you only want to draw the top half of your adult, simply divide your line into four sections instead of five. Whatever the pose, the same simple rules apply.

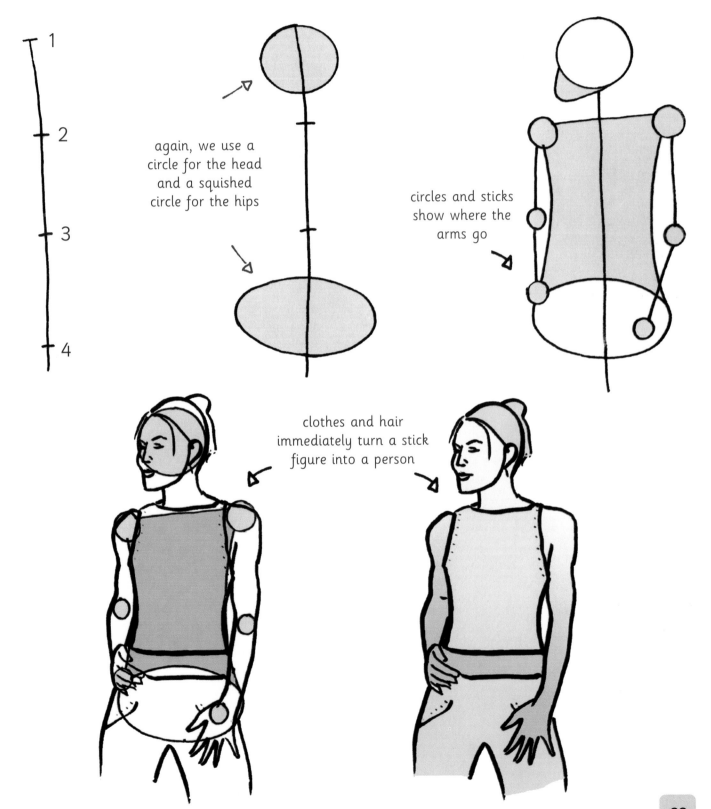

again, we use a circle for the head and a squished circle for the hips

circles and sticks show where the arms go

clothes and hair immediately turn a stick figure into a person

how to draw a moving body

Once the basic technique has been grasped, you'll soon be able to draw figures performing a whole range of movement.

The important thing is always to refer to the movement line – the shape of this will vary according to the action you want to convey.

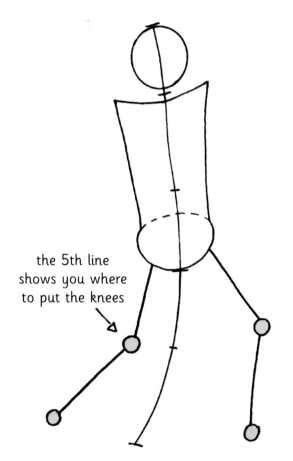

as usual, the 6 dividing lines act as a rough guide ➔ to where the body and limbs should be placed

the 5th line shows you where to put the knees

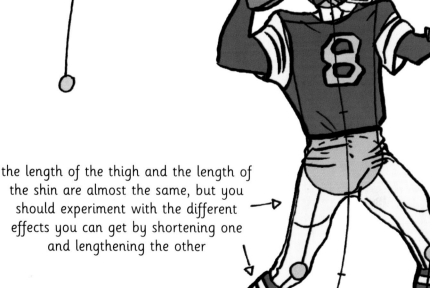

the length of the thigh and the length of the shin are almost the same, but you should experiment with the different ➔ effects you can get by shortening one and lengthening the other

the movement line is very important in helping you work out the spacing of the limbs and body

notice how, for this movement, the thigh is shorter than the shin

Here is the body performing a more exaggerated move. This is more difficult to draw, but you can still do it by using the step-by-step rules.

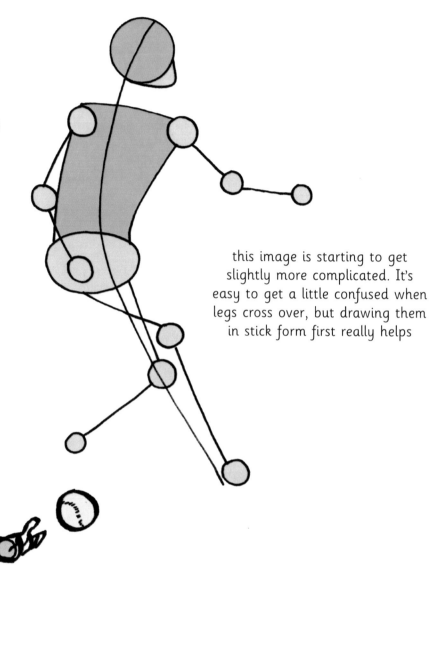

this image is starting to get slightly more complicated. It's easy to get a little confused when legs cross over, but drawing them in stick form first really helps

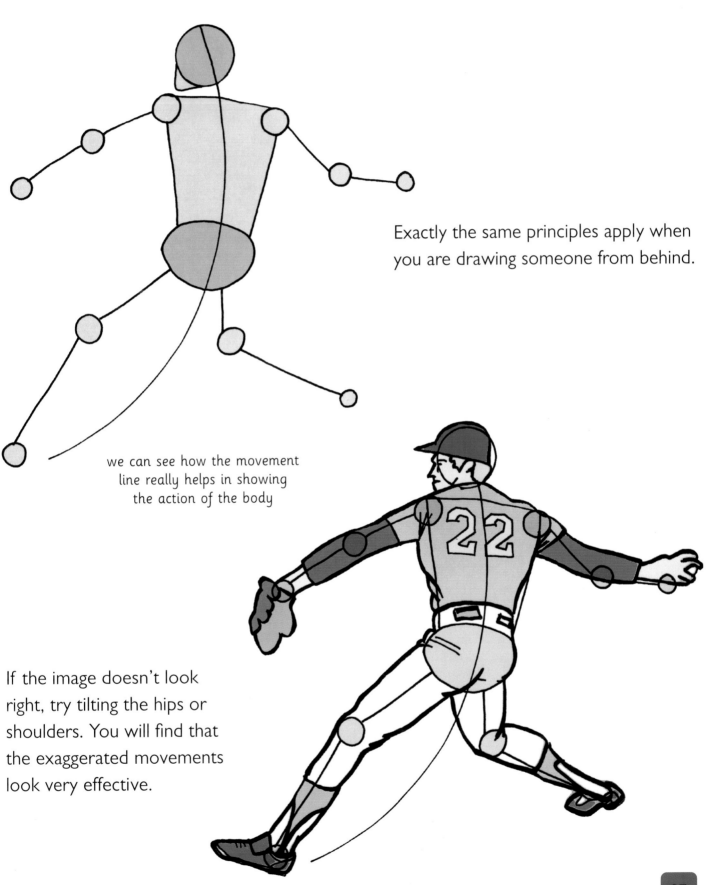

Exactly the same principles apply when you are drawing someone from behind.

we can see how the movement line really helps in showing the action of the body

If the image doesn't look right, try tilting the hips or shoulders. You will find that the exaggerated movements look very effective.

Here are some stick figures in action.
Can you tell what they are doing?

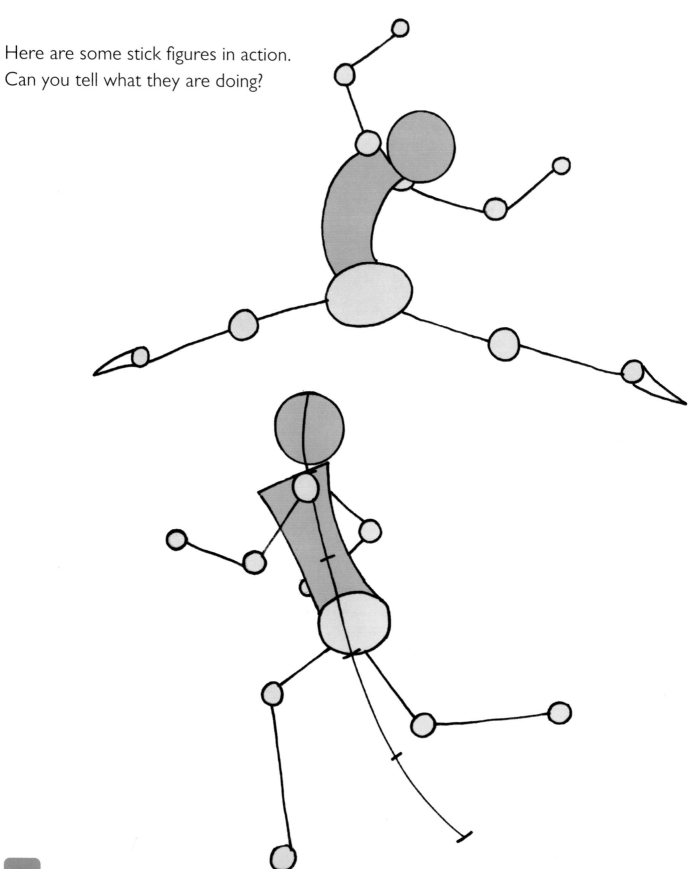

Play around and have a go at drawing some yourself. It's fun and you will be surprised at how easy it is to get effective, yet realistic bodies performing strange and exciting movements!

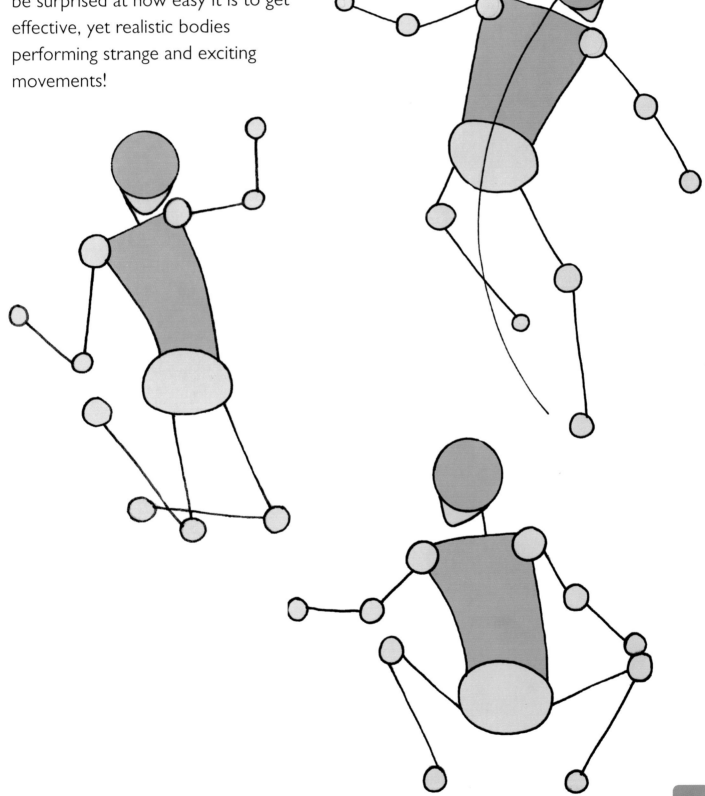

how to draw a cartoon face

Drawing cartoons is great fun and it's easy too! So let's begin!

Stage 1– Draw an oval for the face.

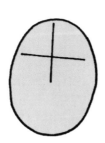 

Stage 2 – Add the hair and draw two small circles for the eyes. Use a cross as a guide if you need to.

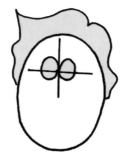 

Stage 3 – Now add the nose and a curved line for the smile.

Have fun experimenting with different hairstyles.

different male hairstyles

different female hairstyles

If you want to change your cartoon character's expression, all you have to do is mess around with the eyes or mouth.

Here are some examples:

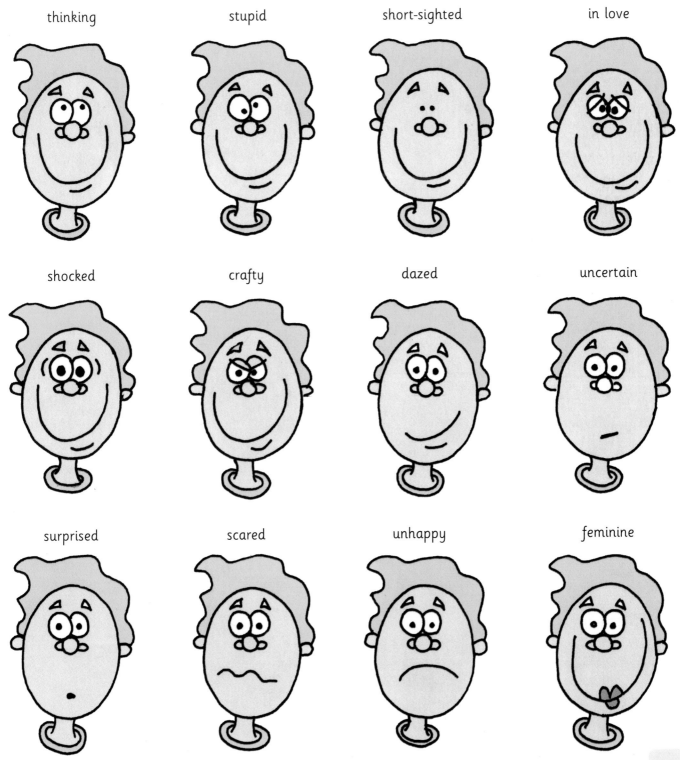

thinking   stupid   short-sighted   in love

shocked   crafty   dazed   uncertain

surprised   scared   unhappy   feminine

how to draw more cartoon faces

Now that you have mastered the basics of the human face and its many wonderful expressions, let's have a look at… HEAD SHAPES!

The head can be drawn using an amazing variety of different shapes, e.g. circle, pear, diamond, triangle, even rectangle! Here are a few examples.

Notice that the nose tends to echo the shape of the head: a rectangular head has an angular nose, a circular head has a round pug nose and so on…

Pear shape:

Circle shape:

Rectangle shape:

Squished circle shape:

Diamond shape:

how to draw a cartoon body

The wonderful thing about a cartoon body is that it can be any size you want. But I think the easiest and best way to start off is to use the three head rule!

The 'three head rule' simply means that the figure is the height of three heads on top of each other.

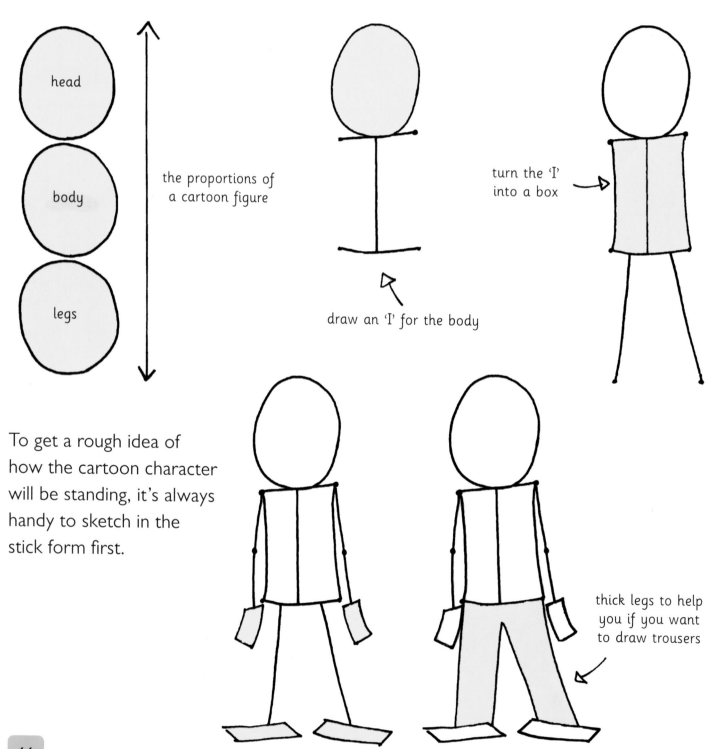

head

body

legs

the proportions of a cartoon figure

draw an 'I' for the body

turn the 'I' into a box

To get a rough idea of how the cartoon character will be standing, it's always handy to sketch in the stick form first.

thick legs to help you if you want to draw trousers

Now all you have to do is think about what you want your cartoon character to look like.

As you can see, all the people on the page have exactly the same body and face shape. It's the clothes and hair that change the person's look.

how to draw cartoon movement

If you got the basics of drawing a moving human figure, then there's good news: drawing moving cartoon figures is even easier!

Again, the thing to remember is to draw the character's movement in stick form first. If it looks right in stick form, then it will look right as a cartoon character. Just add clothes and hair, and you have yourself a moving cartoon figure!

bends for when the elbows and knees are bent

the arms and legs are about the same length

body language can be just as expressive as the face

if there is a stretch, it's always indicated by the shape of the box. The rest of the body's proportions stay the same